Published by CWR, Waverley Abbey House, Waverley Lane, Farnham, Surrey GU9 8EP.
The right of Jonathan Lee to be identified as the author and illustrator of this work has
been asserted by him in accordance with the Copyright, Designs and Patents Act 1988.

See back of book for list of National Distributors.

Concept development, editing, design and production by CWR.

Illustrations: Jonathan Lee

Printed in Spain by Zure

ISBN: 1-85345-317-X

...Remember The First Christmas

Written and illustrated by Jonathan Lee

It was Christmas time and everyone was very excited. Mrs Phips had a special story to tell, in fact, **the greatest story** ever told. She cleared her throat, 'Uh hem', and began to read.

There was once a young lady who lived in a town called Nazareth. She was a lovely, kind and honest person who served God in all she did. Her name was Mary.

NAZARETH

There was an event in Mary's life that was to change the lives of every person who ever lived. The angel Gabriel visited her telling her she would have a son. He was to be born the Son of God, to save His people from sin and His kingdom would have no end.

Remember the Parables

Jonathan Lee presents well-loved parables in a unique blend of watercolour illustrations and text, which will delight children and adults alike.

For children aged 3 to 6 years old.

36 pages

The Wise and Foolish Builders
ISBN: 1-85345-303-X

The Good Samaritan
ISBN: 1-85345-301-3

The Lost Sheep
ISBN: 1-85345-302-1

£3.99
Each (plus p&p)

JESUS WAS BORN TO SAVE US

National Distributors

UK: (and countries not listed below)
CWR, Waverley Abbey House, Waverley Lane, Farnham, Surrey GU9 8EP.
Tel: (01252) 784700 Outside UK +44 (0)1252 784700

AUSTRALIA: CMC Australasia, PO Box 519, Belmont, Victoria 3216.
Tel: (03) 5241 3288

CANADA: Cook Communications Ministries, PO Box 98, 55 Woodslee Avenue, Paris, Ontario.
Tel: 1800 263 2664

GHANA: Challenge Enterprises of Ghana, PO Box 5723, Accra.
Tel: (021) 222437/223249 Fax: (021) 226227

HONG KONG: Cross Communications Ltd, 1/F, 562A Nathan Road, Kowloon.
Tel: 2780 1188 Fax: 2770 6229

INDIA: Crystal Communications, 10-3-18/4/1, East Marredpalli, Secunderabad – 500026. Andhra
Pradesh, Tel/Fax: (040) 27737145

KENYA: Keswick Books and Gifts Ltd, PO Box 10242, Nairobi.
Tel: (02) 331692/226047 Fax: (02) 728557

MALAYSIA: Salvation Book Centre (M) Sdn Bhd, 23 Jalan SS 2/64, 47300 Petaling Jaya, Selangor.
Tel: (03) 78766411/78766797 Fax: (03) 78757066/787 360

NEW ZEALAND: CMC Australasia, PO Box 36015, Lower Hutt.
Tel: 0800 449 408 Fax: 0800 449 049

NIGERIA: FBFM, Helen Baugh House, 96 St Finbarr's College Road, Akoka, Lagos.
Tel: (01) 7747429/4700218/825775/827264

PHILIPPINES: OMF Literature Inc, 776 Boni Avenue, Mandaluyong City.
Tel: (02) 531 2183 Fax: (02) 531 1960

REPUBLIC OF IRELAND: Scripture Union, 40 Talbot Street, Dublin 1.
Tel: (01) 8363764

SINGAPORE: Armour Publishing Pte Ltd, Block 203A Henderson Road, 11–06 Henderson Industrial
Park, Singapore 159546.
Tel: 6 276 9976 Fax: 6 276 7564

SOUTH AFRICA: Struik Christian Books, 80 MacKenzie Street, PO Box 1144, Cape Town 8000.
Tel: (021) 462 4360 Fax: (021) 461 3612

SRI LANKA: Christombu Books, 27 Hospital Street, Colombo 1.
Tel: (01) 433142/328909

TANZANIA: CLC Christian Book Centre, PO Box 1384, Mkwepu Street, Dar es Salaam.
Tel/Fax (022) 2119439

USA: Cook Communications Ministries, PO Box 98, 55 Woodslee Avenue, Paris, Ontario, Canada.
Tel: 1800 263 2664

ZIMBABWE: Word of Life Books, Shop 4, Memorial Building, 35 S Machel Avenue, Harare.
Tel: (04) 781305 Fax: (04) 774739

For email addresses, visit the CWR website: www.cwr.org.uk

CWR is a registered charity – number 294387

..."He will be called...

..."Wonderful counsellor",

"Mighty God",

"Everlasting father",

"Prince of Peace".

MEMORY VERSE
"for there is nothing
that God cannot do."
Luke Ch. 1 v 37

Remember The ~ ~ First Christmas

 Isaiah Ch.9 v6 → Help the shepherds find out more about the birth of Jesus by filling in the missing [words] and letters ~~~~~~~~

v6 "A [⬚] is [born] to us! ~

A [son] is [given] [to] us! ~

And [govern-] will be [upon] [his shoulder] ...

COLOUR ~ IN ~ PAGES!

That night, however, Joseph was told in a dream that he should marry Mary. The child was not to be born of any man but by the Spirit of God. He was to be called Jesus.

This was all rather a surprise to a carpenter called Joseph, Mary's husband-to-be. Joseph knew the child was not his and so thought it would be best to quietly call the marriage off.

STARTING OUT

DIGGERS

MEG GREVE

CREATIVE EDUCATION • CREATIVE PAPERBACKS

CONT

'ENTS

I SEE A DIGGER.

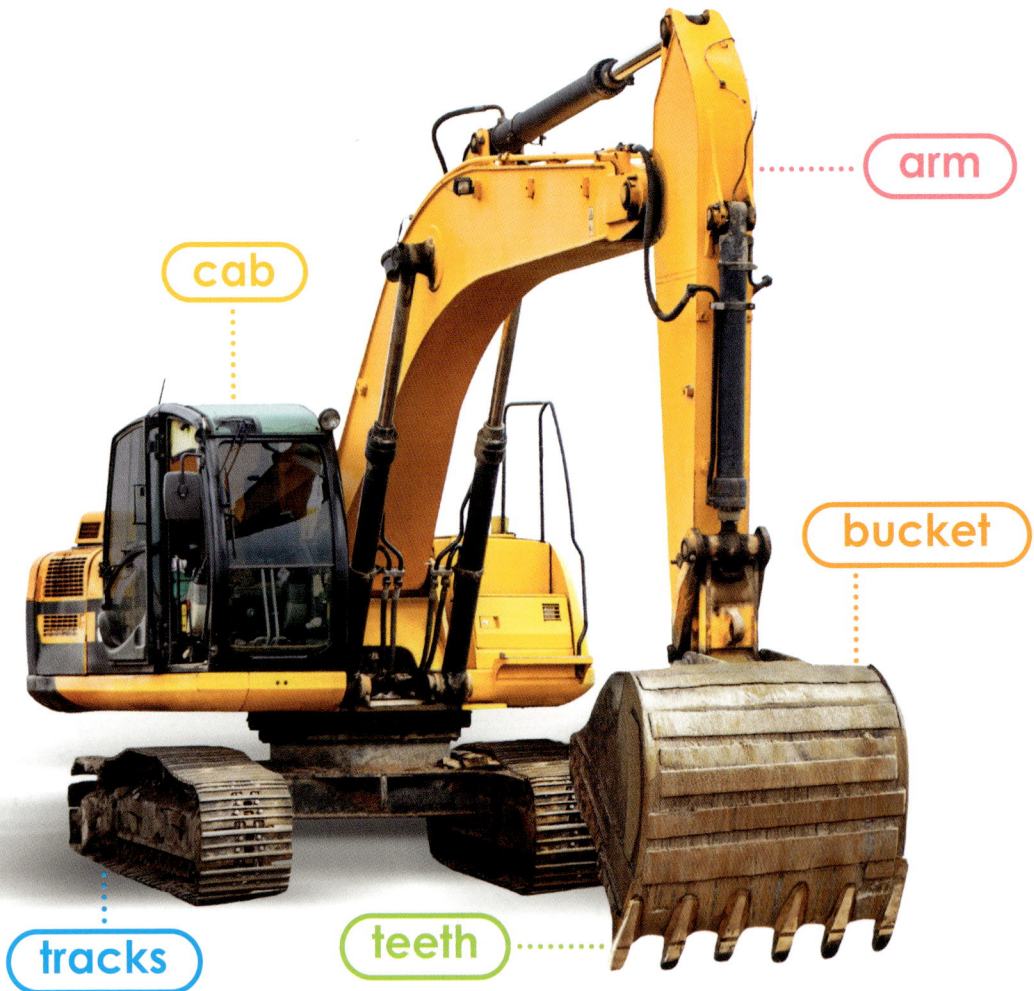

arm

cab

bucket

tracks

teeth

It is also called an excavator.

It is time to work! I might watch a digger on a construction site.

Pull the stick. Up goes the arm!
Push the stick. Down goes the arm!

I see a digger push **rocks**.

I see a digger scoop to
pull in rocks.

A digger lifts, moves, and clears.

A **digger** **can** load a truck.

Diggers are powerful. They can lift 10,000 pounds (4,500 kilograms).

That is about as much as an elephant!

MAKE A
NOISE

WHIR

RRRRR!

Can you make the sounds of a digger?

Listen to these sounds:

https://www.youtube.com/watch?v=z7xT13m00iY

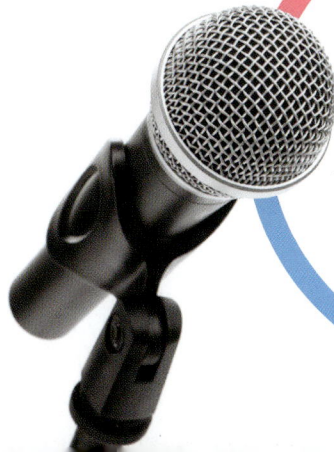

Now it is your turn!

13

DIGGER WORDS

construction site: a place where things are being built

excavator: a machine used to dig into the ground and move dirt and other heavy materials

pull: to move closer

push: to move farther away

READING CORNER

Askew, Amanda. *Diggers*. Richmond Hill, Ont., Canada: Firefly Books, 2010.

Bailey, Annie. *10 Little Excavators*. New York: Doubleday Books for Young Readers, 2022.

Trebbien, Kolbi. *The Tracks on the Excavator*. Washington, D.C.: Blue Balloon Books, 2023.

INDEX

PUBLISHED BY CREATIVE EDUCATION AND CREATIVE PAPERBACKS
P.O. Box 227, Mankato, Minnesota 56002
Creative Education and Creative Paperbacks
are imprints of The Creative Company
www.thecreativecompany.us

LIBRARY OF CONGRESS CATALOGING-IN-PUBLICATION DATA
Names: Greve, Meg, author.
Title: Diggers / by Meg Greve.
Description: Mankato, Minnesota : Creative Education
  and Creative Paperbacks, [2025] | Series: Starting out
  | Includes bibliographical references and index. |
  Audience: Ages 4-7 | Audience: Grades K-1 | Summary:
  "Diggers will introduce budding book learners to a noisy,
  colorful world with this new Starting Out title. Colorful
  photos, labeled diagrams, 'Make a Noise' section,
  glossary, and more ignite a passion for learning"--
  Provided by publisher.
Identifiers: LCCN 2023059426 (print) | LCCN 2023059427
  (ebook) | ISBN 9798889891703 (library binding) | ISBN
  9781682775554 (paperback) | ISBN 9798889891826
  (ebook)
Subjects: LCSH: Excavating machinery--Juvenile literature.
  | Earthmoving machinery--Juvenile literature. | CYAC:
  Excavating machinery. | Earthmoving machinery. |
  LCGFT: Instructional and educational works.
Classification: LCC TA732 .G74 2025 (print) | LCC TA732
  (ebook) | DDC 621.8/65--dc23/eng/20240128
LC record available at https://lccn.loc.gov/2023059426
LC ebook record available at https://lccn.loc.
  gov/2023059427

DESIGN AND PRODUCTION
Design by Rhea Magaro
Production by Beeline Media and Design
Art direction by Tom Morgan
Printed in the United States of America

PHOTOGRAPHS by Alamy (Peter Righteous), Getty Images (ollo, Antagain), Shutterstock (artoflogic, freestore 839, Another77, Filmfoto, Comaniciu Dan, Krashenitsa Dmitrii, mark gusev, Patryk Kosmider, Bohbeh, Mr. Tempter)